GREAT SCOTTISH RECIPES

From The Laird's Scots Larder

Published by Lang Syne Publishers Ltd
45 Finnieston St., Glasgow
Tel: 041-204 3104
Printed by Dave Barr Print
45 Finnieston Street, Glasgow
Tel: 041-221 2598

Reprinted 1992

Peace & plenty

INTRODUCTION

The title of this book betrays something of its function. It is not a cookery book, although I have included a representative selection of distinctively Scottish recipes. Nor is it a work of scholarship, although I hope scholars will not find too much of substance to complain of in its pages. If they do, I shall plead the demands of compression in mitigation, for that has been my purpose, to compress within narrow and managable scope, a survey of the rich variety of the Scottish way with the food of its larder.

It has been my good fortune to spend a quarter of a century professionally engaged in observing and recording the Scottish food scene — what and how it is produced, what and how it is eaten and how it is distributed — for an indulgent employer, the British Farm Produce Council. It is the Council which has allowed me the experience which is the raw material of this book, and while not wishing on it any responsibility for the views I express, I am grateful to the Council for making it possible for me to do so.

I have been fortunate in other ways. The twenty-five years in which I have lived and worked in Scotland have seen a vigorous renascence in the traditions of the Scottish Kitchen. A remarkable number of the best cookery writers of the age have been Scots, at once born of, and nourishing that renascence, and I have been privileged to know personally, or correspond with, many of them. Two in particular I wish to name. The latest star in this particular firmament is surely Catherine Brown. Over the years she has been variously my assistant and colleague. With the recent publication of her "Scottish Cookery" she has assumed the role of mentor. Secondly, though by far first in time, F. Marian MacNeil was not only the literary inspiration of my own interest in the subject, but also, through her "The Scots Kitchen", that of the whole renascence of Scottish *cuisine.*

I ask of my readers only that they are open to the enthusiasm which has been my pleasure as well as my work. That is what I hope to share with them in these pages. To those who are free, willing and able, I suggest that they emulate — for I cannot and will not share — the most central piece of my good fortune, to have married the superb Highland cook to whom I have dedicated this book.

"I am na fou, I just hae plenty"

Chapter One

The Land

A nation's history, its culture, and no less its Larder, proceed primarily from its land and the relationship of its People to its Land. In Scotland's case, circumstance has given that truism a special force, only with the proviso that it is also the encircling sea which has been crucial.

What is this land of Scotland? Is it big or small, rich or poor? Above all, it is HARD: physically hard, structured of rock, for the most part old hard rock and including in its remote North West, some of the most ancient rocks known on Earth. It is a land, too, which is hard in the demands it makes on those who live from it, often thin of soil, unsuited to the agricultural exploitation which has, since Neolithic times, been the only source of Mankind's advance.

As to size, Scots themselves suffer from some confusion about their Land, so why should not others? Even Britain as a whole likes to perceive itself as the "tight little Island", the small centre of a great worldwide Power, in trade if no longer in Empire. And Scots understandably take the concept a stage further by comparing Scotland's small extent with that of its large and often dominating neighbour to the South. From that flows the passion which "Little Scotland" carries to modern sporting encounters, never mind the bloodier ones of every recorded century save the last two!

And yet, on anything less than the continental scale of the U.S., Canada, Russia and the like, Scotland is by no means small. It is narrow; I myself regularly drive across it, from its near-empty Atlantic coast where our Western neighbours are the Americas, to the North Sea across which the heartland of Europe is imminent. And I often do so after dinner! But going from North to South it is a different matter. A day's journey will not span it, and the traveller would be hard put to it to traverse only its Mainland part by even the swiftest of land-based transport systems in 24 hours.

Latitude best spells out this North-South spread of Scotland. That of Galloway and Gretna Green is about 55 North; that of Shetland over 60. It is a difference in latitude which can be compared with that between Long Island and Newfoundland, between Sydney and Brisbane, or with the width of the Mediterranean Sea, from its African to its European shores.

Latitude says something else profoundly significant about the land of Scotland. It is a Northern Land. Each of those comparisons I have offered lies far closer to the Equator than does Scotland's southernmost point. Edinburgh shares its northerly latitude with Labrador, Prince Rupert, and Moscow; Shetland with Anchorage, Cape Farewell, and Leningrad. In the Southern Hemisphere no land at all save the appropriately named South Shetlands interrupts the globe-circling icy wastes of the Antarctic Ocean. Happily for the Scots, the moderating influence of the Atlantic displaces direct climatic analogies from these extreme latitudes, but they do confer inescapable characteristics of winter dark and summer light, and even of stark climatic contrasts between seasons, which are unknown in more equatorially placed lands.

Scotland is also a wet land. Only rarely, and only on its sheltered Eastern side, does Scotland lack for water in its soils. West of its great Central Massif, it is all too copiously provided with rain laden winds from the ocean. These rains fall on a thinly soiled land, on glen-riven hills and mountains, steep and rocky, to make grass and forest almost everywhere the only possible crop, and hardy livestock, feral and domestic alike, the only possible means of exploitation.

On the Central Massif — the Grampians, the Western Highlands and those of the North-West, conditions are often too severe even for this limited range of economic activities. For all that their height rarely exceeds what elsewhere would be an unremarkable 1000 metres, the combination of that height with northerly latitude and bareness of terrain creates a climate and ecology for which Alpine, Arctic and Tundra are proper descriptions. Here even the hardiest of hill-walkers proceeds with circumspection, and only the Shepherd, the Forester and the Gamekeeper pursues his daily calling.

From these high places there rushes an unending flow of ground water, filling and over-filling the ice-gouged lochs, and feeding the great rivers of Scotland's eastern lowlands — Spey, Isla, Dee, Don, Tay, Earn and Forth, which deepen and widen as they flow through broad straths until they reach the North Sea in their firths. Here the land is in dramatic contrast with that to the west, the soil deep and fertile, the terrain gentler and flatter, yet both watered and well drained in the sedimentary geology of Scotland south and east of the Highland Line running from Peterhead to Helensburgh.

Around this land I have so far described lies the never distant Sea, both threatening and sustaining the necklace of communities which live by it, a richly provided, if over-exploited sea. But to the South lie lands which are themselves marked off from those still farther South, by yet another Upland barrier, not high by continental standards, but both bleak and beautiful

The Cheviots and their outliers have been Scotland's historic bastion against the encroachments of the English, nursery of men as hard and durable as the very stone of which Scotland is formed, and nursery of a great wealth of stock and stockmen — refuge too, in troublous Old Time. It is a country riven by deep valleys whose water was to engine the woollen industries founded on the sheep of these hills. Foremost among these waters is the eponymous Tweed, a characteristically Scottish river, even if an accident of history has given its final few sea-bound miles to England.

Only one quarter remains, the South West, the land of Dumfries and Galloway and Robert Burns' Ayrshire. It is a quarter which contains within itself many of the contrasting peculiarites of Scotland as a whole — dour peaty high moors, the broad dales of Annan and Nith, the gentle and mild coastlands of Solway and Galloway, and the rich pastures of broad Ayrshire, home of Scotland's native breed of dairy cattle. And here in Ayrshire, it brings us full circle to the Highlands of Argyll across the great inland sea of the Outer Firth of Clyde.

Here then, set down no doubt all too briefly, is the essential nature of this unique land of the Scots. No mention here of its great and varied beauty, none of its three marvellous adjacent archipelagoes, Shetland, Orkney and the Hebrides, haunted in the North by Viking memories and in the West by those of the most anciently literate of Europe's peoples, the Gaels. This is the land which has coloured the plenishing of the Larder and the furnishing of the Table.

"Hech! Sirs — I'll rive"

Chapter Two

The Larder

All the characteristics of the Land — its chemistry, its geology, its form, its structure, its topography and even its ownership — combine in a myriad ways to limit and determine what Man can conjure from it for his benefit. Even the climate is secondary to the innate opportunities presented by the soil itself. But climate and the land also interact with each other in determining how and to what extent the land is productive, and within Scotland's modest compass, that interaction is complex in the varied results it generates.

There are but two routes into Scotland, taken by Roman invaders and later more welcome visitors alike, the East and the West. The Eastern route divides before the Border to give a choice between the flat and easy coastland route through Berwick, and the long climb up the bare moorlands of Northumberland to enter Scotland over the Cheviots at Carter Bar and so into the lush pastures of the Middle Tweed. In the West, Carlisle sits on the Roman Wall and all to the North is Scotland, the route only then dividing to take the clefts of the Annan or the Nith towards Glasgow and the Clyde crossing, or swinging eastwards towards the Upper Tweed and so to the woollen towns of Tweedsdale, and the eastern entry.

Such a description ignores the great triangle of land lying between Nithsdale and the Firth of Clyde, the historic counties of Dumfries, Wigtown and Ayrshire, and the Stewartry of Kirkcudbright which have for over two centuries been the home of Scotland's Dairy industry, the home too, of its only native Dairy Breed, the Ayrshire. The farming land here is strung around a core of high and ungenerous hills now much given over to forestry. But in the dales and on the coastlands are alluvial lands, well watered by abundant rain, and for the most part favoured by mild winters, comparable, indeed with those of that other great dairying area in South-West England, far, far to the South. It is a land of milk and butter and of cheese. The latter may at first sight seem something of an interloper, for it is preeminently Cheddar Cheese that is made here.

Yet the Cheddar process was established in Ayrshire two hundred years ago and even that long ago was being modified and developed in a distinctively Scottish way. And a hundred years before that, a similar process produced Dunlop cheese in the Ayrshire village of that name, a name now largely reserved for the speciality hard cheeses produced in the Northern and Western Isles.

Historically, pig husbandry is often associated with milk production — Denmark and Wiltshire are egregious examples. And it was so in Ayrshire. In a world in which the Wiltshire Bacon Cure has become all but universal, the Ayrshire Cure, correctly a dry cure of the separate and de-boned joints, unlike the whole-sided Wiltshire brine method, produces a milder bacon and the characteristically rolled form which remains the preferred choice of Scottish housewives. It also produces some confusion for the unwary visitor, for in Scotland, "ham" tends to mean bacon, and "Gammon" boiled ham!

Eastward of the Dairy country of South-West Scotland lie the high grassy hills of the Borders. These were turbulent lands, disputed between the Scottish and English jurisdictions until the dawn of the Modern Age and the union of the Crowns, nurturing a piratical society in which wealth was expressed in terms of stock, particularly beef cattle. Only in the Eighteenth Century did the abundant water power and the Industrial Revolution meet in the prosperity of the woollen towns along the Tweed and other rivers. Sheep, anciently the source of monastic wealth in the Eastern Borders — Melrose, Roxburgh and others — returned in enhanced numbers and improved quality, to join the improving cattle of that Improving Century. The native Cheviot sheep, and the Border Leicester developed from the work of the first of the livestock improvers, James Brindley, have gone on to be the foundation, with the Blackface of the West, of the National Flock which two centuries on, now numbers approaching 10,000,000 at the peak of the season.

Scottish sheepmeat, always a large element in the national diet, has not achieved, as yet, the international renown of Scotch beef, and yet it is today among the foremost resources of the Scottish economy. Production is over twice as great as consumption at home, and more than

England seeks the bounty — lawfully now, by way of trade! Sheep-keeping in Scotland is almost everywhere an extensive business, making use of wide expanses of hill and upland, and these natural methods of production make Scotch lamb a sought-after commodity in Europe and beyond, where it is beginning to achieve the same sort of reputation long enjoyed by Scotch beef.

Still further East the lonely hills give way to the Merselands of the lower Tweed, the first-encountered of Scotland's arable lands which sweep North and East along both sides of the broad Firth of Forth and on beyond that of the Tay, until in Kincardineshire and Aberdeenshire, they are squeezed almost into the North Sea by the shoulder-thrust of the Eastern Grampian Mountains. From this fertile belt, the Larder is well charged with a wide variety of crops, all grown in varying proportions throughout its length. Cereals, traditionally mainly Barley and Oats but nowadays equally Wheat, are everywhere. But some areas have become specialised over the generations, perhaps because of soil or climate, but as patently because of inherited and transmitted skills. Vegetables of many kinds have long been the province of the Lothians to the East of Edinburgh, and in particular, leeks, of the Musselburgh shore. That specialism has spread widely across the Forth to the Kingdom of Fife, while across the Tay is the centre of the one crop in which Scotland is pre-eminent in all Europe, raspberries.

Raspberries have grown wild all over Scotland for centuries, and are to be found in great perfection of taste even in the wild places of the West. But in the Carse, or alluvial plain, of Gowrie between Perth and Dundee, some accident of soil and skill has centred the greatest concentration of commercial growing of the fruit, which still today produces some three-quarters of the U.K. crop, and two-thirds of that of the Common Market.

The modern growing industry was founded around Blairgowrie, surprisingly recently, in the closing years of the last Century, and until only a couple of decades ago was the milieu of a rich fund of folk lore and song built on the annual picking migration of workers around the raspberry fields, comparable with the exodus of East Enders to the hop fields of Kent. Modern plant varieties and cultural methods have largely spread the harvesting peak to obviate the mass picking of the "berrying". Although mechanical harvesting has not yet arrived, as it has in the case of the hops, it is no accident that the Scottish Plant Research Institute at Invergowrie, established in the heart of the fruit growing area, is involved with its development, as well as with the development of new varieties, and indeed, new hybrid fruits such as the Tayberry and the Tummelberry. The "Glen" series of raspberry varieties were bred at the Institute, Glen Clova has long been the principal commercial variety, now joined by Glen Prosen. Both have proved well adapted to the latest development in the industry, free-flow freezing. Handled carefully, the raspberry uniquely emerges from the deep-freeze with its form and taste unimpaired, an adornment to any table at any time of the year.

Further North, horticultural interest was traditionally centred not on supplying the Larder but the flower vase. Aberdeen is not only a city of beef but of roses, and the small, mountainous county of Banff even further North, still produces much of the United Kingdom's hardy nursery stock. In Kincardineshire and Aberdeenshire, this interest has been more than maintained with bulbs from the area being exported to the home of the tulip, Holland. But the same skills are demanded by fruit growing and these areas, with the adjacent Morayshire, grow some of the finest berry fruits in Scotland — raspberries, but also late harvested strawberries of particular excellence, perhaps the result of the longer growing period imposed by the Northern latitiude.

Perhaps that characteristic of latitude also accounts for the special quality of Scottish tomatoes, grown mainly in the glasshouse area of the middle Clyde valley. This was always a growing area thanks to its proximity to the busy markets of Glasgow and Edinburgh. Once the area concentrated on apples and plums, and on strawberries, but now only a few plums, admittedly of spectacular quality, remain. They have been replaced by salad crops, especially tomatoes of particular sweetness and firmness of texture. But even that crop is grown in the North East as well, in one case using waste heat from that region's foremost gastronomic gift to the World, Whisky.

No part of Scotland can be excluded from the Whisky story, and no superlative is too extreme in its telling. Some strange magical alchemy of atmosphere, water and grain has made Scotch the world's most sought after spirit, Scotland's most valuable export, and, alas, the United Kingdom's apparently most inexhaustible of Revenue sources! Its story is both too long and too complex to be retold here. Let it suffice to say that great subtleties distinguish the whisky of one Distillery from that of even its closest neighbour; that peat smoke and the water of the Hills contribute their essence to its final perfection; and that while it is in the North-east that distilleries of malt whisky most proliferate, it is two hundred miles and more to the

South-west in the Islands of the Western Sea, and especially on Islay, that the most distinctive and egregious flavours are conjured; and that, of the four great families of Scotch Malt Whisky generally recognised — Lowland Malt, Strathspey Malt, Highland Malt and Island Malt — none receives the palm from the present writer! For there is a fifth family, sadly now reduced to only two representatives, Campbeltown, which is as different from its robust near-neighbour in Islay as from its refined more distant ones in Strathspey, but which has an appeal of its own, not least for its magnificent "nose."

Campbeltown is on Kintyre, hanging like a long pendant from the beautiful and mountainous county of Argyll, and so confronts across the mighty Firth of Clyde, the fertile Southwestern dairy lands where this rapid circuit of Scotland's land began. Yet the three most central of the historical provisions of the Scots Larder, have escaped all notice in this circuit. They are Oats, Beef and Potatoes. Oats' omission is best ascribed to its ubiquitous presence in farm, larder and table. In extent and production, it is now a tiny proportion of Scottish cereal production yet grown everywhere, from broad arable acres in the East to tiny hand-reaped crofts in the West. And when the focus is shifted from the Larder to the Kitchen, it will become clear how central oats are to the story of Scottish food.

Beef and potatoes are different matters, for they do have their particular areas of specialisation, albeit ones that are varied and widespread. Oddly, part of the story of each belongs to that same South-West where the circuit began. Great quantities of potatoes are grown on the arable farms of the Lothians, Fife, Angus and Kincardineshire, and in the central county of Scotland, Perth, which bestrides the Highland line and contains a bit of all Scotland within its wide bounds. But it is in the South-West, in Wigtown and Ayrshire, that the Scottish Early Potato has been grown for the past 100 years. Indeed, the visitor to Scotland in June and July will see everywhere greengrocers' notices proclaiming the arrival of "Ayrshires" as though it was a particular variety! What was traditionally implied was in truth a particular variety, the Epicure much beloved, especially in the populous West of Scotland. But there are many varieties, if not unknown abroad, less favoured than at home in Scotland, like Golden Wonder, the sans pareil of boiling potatoes in the latter part of the season, floury and strong skinned, or Kerrs Pinks, an all-rounder full of flavour. The soil in which a potato is grown is at least as important as its variety, and if the writer's favourite whisky comes from the remote South-West, his favourite potato is one grown diagonally across Scotland in the Black Isle. It is a variety not greatly liked in Scotland, the King Edward, but one widely grown for the English market, and it reaches perfection in the deep rich glacial soil of the Black Isle — not in truth an island, but almost so, lying North of Inverness between the Beauly and the Cromarty Firths.

And so there remains only beef of the land's great gifts to the larder. Again the South-West of Scotland plays its part, contributing another native breed of cattle, the Galloway. Like the more famous Aberdeen-Angus, it is black and hornless, but its special quality is extreme hardiness and thriftiness, which enables it to live and thrive on the ungenerous forage it finds on its native hills, as it does in similarly rigorous conditions around the World. It is one of the four native beef breeds of Scotch beef cattle, the Aberdeen-Angus, the Shorthorn, the Galloway and the Highland, each of which has been improved and refined by skilled breeding over two centuries, and by an exceptional facility in stockmanship which has been the hallmark of many generations of Scottish farmers. Both the skill and the stock have been among the foremost of Scottish exports over those centuries, and have left their marks in the herds of every temperate region of the Globe.

The excellence of the stock is matched by that of the final product offered in Scottish butchers' shops. The visitor may first be struck by the higher prices paid at home, compared with those for "Scotch Beef" south of the Border and beyond. For there is scarcely a butcher in England who does not boast of selling "Finest Scotch Beef." Some, much, may well have come from Scotland, for as with Lamb, production far outstrips domestic demand. But if all the "Scotch" beef sold as such came in fact from Scotland, the country would long since have sunk, mountains and all, beneath the weight of beeves on the hoof! The "Scotch" can only refer to the blood of those Scotch breeds which are used so widely to confer quality on herds of less notable pedigree. At home it is, as it were, the pure milk of the word which is demanded by the discriminating housewife, served by a system and quality of butchery which is more demanding of time and skill than that generally found in England, more akin to the Continental butchery of dissection. Hence the higher prices. But hence too the superior quality of satisfaction revealed by closer acquaintance. It is a quality which can be sought and found all over Scotland. The Aberdeen-Angus, the most refined beef producer of them all, has its home typically in the two counties of its name, but also on the marvellous pastures of Strathmore in Perthshire and in the Merse of Tweed. But they are also to be found, along with the three other breeds, in any part of Scotland, even in the more favoured parts of the Highlands whose main role in meat production is, by complex cross-breeding, to act as a great pool of much sought-after young stock reared for finishing on the lusher pastures of the Lowlands.

The Land so plenishes the Larder. So does the Sea, and the waters of river and loch. There is, after all, a lot of sea. The coastline is deeply indented, in some instances by many scores of miles, and that of Argyll alone is said to exceed that of all France. And right round the coast, from Eyemouth with its back door almost in English Berwick, past the East Neuk towns of Fife, Arbroath of the Smokies, Aberdeen and the fisher villages of Buchan and the Moray Firth, to the far North at Wick and farther still to Shetland, and then West and South again by way of the Minch, the Western Isles to the Mull of Kintyre, the Firth of Clyde, and to Solway, there is a garland of fishing communities wresting their dangerous living from the encircling Sea. Some are large towns like Peterhead and Fraserburgh in the North-East or Oban in the West, one even a city, Aberdeen, though there fishing has been supplanted by other activities in the stormy North Sea.

The very proliferation of these communities, itself speaks of the abundance of fish available to Scotland's Larder. Some 70% of the United Kingdom catch is now landed at Scottish ports, and beyond those landings are the thousands of tonnes transferred afloat to factory ships from Eastern Europe. It is an ancient trail these seekers after Scottish fish follow. In the Middle Ages, long before Scotland could look South for trade with impunity, she faced towards the Baltic with the export of vast numbers of salted herring, and Amsterdam is reputedly founded — physically or commercially — on the bones of Scottish herring!

Herring is at the heart of the fish story of Scotland. It was anciently a great source of wealth, and more recently of legend and song around the lives of fishermen and the fisher girls on the quay. The herring reached its highest perfection in our waters. A succession of seasons are marked and delimited by the needs of conservation of stock — North Sea, Shetland, the Minch, and separate from them all, the so-called Loch Fyne herring, more properly that of the Firth of Clyde. Much passion is generated by the comparison of the merits of herring from the various stocks, and indeed whether there are separate and different stocks at all. But few will deny that the Loch Fyne, its flesh a delicate mushroom blush, its whole body plump and succulent, is sui generis, and many, this writer among them, will assert that the Sea has nothing to offer which exceeds the Loch Fyne in subtle magnificence.

Herring is not only the heart of the fish story; it is almost half of it. Amid such an abundance of fish, it can only be because of such riches at the doorstep that Scotland is so narrowly concerned with just two species, herring and haddock. Other fish are caught — and largely ignored by Scottish housewives. Even the magnificent cod is left on the slab if haddock is to be had. But in a further paradox, the Scots, in their extreme conservative taste in fish, have constructed a veritable cornucopia from a single fish, the haddock. There is the whole fish in the round, there are the fillets, there are the steaks. And it is gross simplification to speak merely of Smoked Haddock. There are Arbroath Smokies, small haddock hot-smoked on the bone. There are smoked fillets both pale and dark, London-cut or Aberdeen-cut. And above all there is the true and revered Finnan Haddie, a haddock split but not deboned, and smoked in that form. Again, choice lies between pale and dark, exercised by Scots with much discrimination and care for the mood and style of the intended meal. It is one of the great delicacies of Scotland and has its own wide canon of treatments and cooking methods.

For all that the Scottish tradition in fish is one of great conservatism, recent decades have seen something of a revolution in the exploitation of a sea resource which was ignored for centuries. Inshore waters have always been bountifully supplied with shellfish and molluscs of every sort — no doubt the very first prehistoric Scots found them their only staple. But only since the 1960s has there been any vigorous use made of this abundant supply created by the great expanses of sheltered waters, unpolluted to a degree almost unknown elsewhere in Europe. Clams, shrimps, prawns, all were thrown back as a nuisance to fishermen only a generation ago. It was a fate similarly suffered by the free-est swimming of all fish — mackerel. Now they, along with Lobsters and Crabs, are of great commercial importance, filling many Scots Larders and those of affluent Europe as well.

Not only are the sea-acres of Scotland unpolluted, so too are a fortunate majority of its land-waters in Loch and River. Nature has gifted this resource, and men now exploit it by farming the fish natural to it. Salmon and Sea-trout naturally cross the boundary between salt and fresh water, and farming systems have been developed for both environments, to multiply production, especially of Salmon, every year in the present decade, without revealing any ceiling to future growth. Similarly blessed with plenty of un-polluted fresh water in her lochs, great and small, and swift-flowing rivers, Scotland has seen a phenomenal growth in fish farms, especially in the West and mainly producing Rainbow Trout. And the latest of these farming developments has been the farming of both shellfish and molluscs, especially in the Western Isles.

Nature was not done with Scotland when it gave her the Sea and the Land. There is also the Air, home of at least the feathered form of what is collectively known as Game. Most famously, the High Places are the home of the Red Grouse, so linked to Scotland that its Latin name is L.lagopus scoticus. Below the tree-line there are Blackcock and the spectacular capercailzie, and lower still the less characteristically Scottish pheasant and partridge. In the woods, too, are deer, but it is on the bare hillside that the great Red Deer of Scotland lives wild, and is hunted, not with hounds, but under the arduous tutelege of the skilled Stalking Ghillie, pilot perhaps on stormy loch waters, or guide in the shoals and cataracts of the turbulent salmon and trout rivers. For all its repute and abundance, however, and for all the excellence ensured by Scotland's great tracts of wild-lands, it must be said that, for reasons largely of social history, Game has played only a modest part in her national larder.

THE FISH DINNER.

"THE WHITEBAIT SEEM VERY LARGE, WAITER!"
"YES, SIR; VERY FINE AT PRESENT, SIR."

Chapter Three

The Kitchen

"*K*itchen" is a simple, warm word, describing the very core of the Home. But more than that is implied by its use here. It enshrines the idea that a Nation expresses something of itself in its Kitchen, both recording and celebrating its history, exploiting the goods and talents with which Nature has enriched it, and often nurturing a good conceit of itself. Used in that way, the word kitchen implies more than a mere list of recipes peculiar to the nation, but less than some universal system adopted by its people. Not even the dominant tradition of the "Kitchen", that of France, does that, for its two pre-eminent qualities are its rich regional diversity, and its ready assimilation of the best of food from other countries. The concept, of course, begins with the dishes commonly used, but their assemblage into a corpus illuminates the principles and traditions from which they are derived, so that the whole becomes greater than the separate parts. That is what is implied here by the phrase "The Kitchen"

In common with the rest of the British Isles, the Kitchen in Scotland was little regarded for many centuries, seen as no more than a necessity of survival. A refined and discriminating view of it as an enhancing aspect of life was left to "Foreigners". But for a brief moment, not surprisingly as part of that Golden Age at the end of the Eighteenth and beginning of the Nineteenth Centuries when Scotland led and dominated the intellectual life of Europe, the Scots Kitchen emerged from that blight to be noted, recorded and developed in many different ways. The published Journals of Mrs. Elizabeth Grant of Rothiemurchus record the delights emerging from a kitchen in the then remote Highlands, a profusion of household manuals spread the message through other strata of Scottish society. And this was the climate in which it was possible for Robert Burns, perhaps uniquely, to dignify in the finest of vernacular poesy, a mundane foodstuff in his ode To A Haggis.

There were many manifestations of a new awareness of the Scots Kitchen, but it was the dominant and seminal literary figure of the Age who set the seal on the story. Sir Walter Scott touched most aspects of Scottish life, the Scots Kitchen among them. Among the least of his novels is the little read St. Ronan's Well, but its tale is woven round the Cleikum Club, a diverse group of friends meeting in Meg Dods' hostelry in Innerleithen to enjoy, celebrate — and quarrel over — the delights of the good Meg's cooking. In recounting these delights Scott created a reference point for the Scots Kitchen which was developed in the publication in 1826 of Meg Dods' "The Cook and Housewife's Manual." Its at least ostensible author was Mrs. Elizabeth Johnston (1781-1857), a lady of much talent and wit, but she was certainly inspired to its compilation by her friendship with Sir Walter, and there are some reasons for thinking that Scott himself had a hand in the writing. Be that as it may, the introduction to the Manual carries forward the story of the diners and hostess of the Cleikum as a framework for an account of the Scottish National Dishes accompanied by some sixty recipes. Thus was a benchmark established for the Scottish Kitchen.

Perhaps becausae of the swift dispersal of the ambience of Edinburgh's Golden Age, perhaps because of the social change and urbanisation wrought so massively in Scotland by the Industrial Revolution to which it so largely gave birth, it was a bench-mark substantially lost through the remainder of the Nineteenth Century. Yet two remarkable innovations appeared in Gastronomy in Scotland to testify to a continuing originality in Scottish eating habits; both were in the field of public eating, and both in the provenance of Glasgow rather than Edinburgh. In mid-century, William Lang invented the Sandwich-bar a hundred years before Fast-Food was ever heard of, and by all accounts the road from the Founder to the Imitators has been downhill all the way! Even if Thackeray described Mr. Lang's productions as "fifty ways of spoiling one's dinner", the then Editor of Punch described Lang as "the Napoleon of sandwiches" and waxed eloquent in praise of the hundred varieties Lang's offered. Lang also first introduced "payment by honour" and the establishment continued its practice until its closure as recently as the 1970s, a fact that should give pause to any who seek to denigrate the great and good City of Glasgow.

At the turn of the Century, Kate Cranston presided over another catering innovation which first saw the light of day in Glasgow, the Tea Room. What the coffee house was to

Eighteenth Century male society, Miss Cranston's Tea Rooms were to ladies in Glasgow, from the opening of the first in the City's Argyle Street in 1884. Never before had a place of resort and refreshment for ladies been provided, and perhaps the timing of the idea was significant, for it coincided with what might be called Glasgow's Golden Age, when its commercial vigour was matched by artistic achievements in painting and architecture. Certainly Miss Cranston's Tea Rooms became as famous for the decors designed for them by Charles Rennie MacIntosh as for their food. And for all that Lang's and Cranston's were innovative, neither could be said to have revived interest in any characteristically Scottish Kitchen. That had to wait a further generation, until some unrecorded moment just before 1930. And it was from Meg Dods that the inspiration came.

In the 1920s F.Marian McNeill, then a young anthropologist of distinction, was browsing in an Edinburgh second-hand bookshop when she chanced on a copy of Meg Dods' Manual. She bought it — "idly" she used to say, but her friends know that she was never idle through all her long life. The result was the writing of her "The Scots Kitchen" published originally by Blackie, and now in paperback by Granada. That splendid book is a repository not only of Meg Dods' recipes and those of Marian McNeill's friends and correspondents, but also of her deep feeling for the story of Scotland's people. It, together with a long established tradition of Scottish education in the field, in the Colleges of Domestic Science of Glasgow, Edinburgh and Aberdeen, was the soil from which grew a rich crop of distinguished writers on cookery in the years after World War II. Elizabeth Craig was perhaps the first of these, the latest Catherine Brown, whose distinguished work is more closely concerned with the Scottish Tradition, the Scottish Kitchen, than that of her predecessors since Marian McNeill.

That Scottish Kitchen had its origin many centuries before Meg Dods. It grew as it assimilated influences from other cultures, and from the development of the resources of its own land, but it grew without losing as its core the practices formed by the spartan lives of the people it served. This was a rural nation, a nation of cottages, the Castle a mere on-graft. The cottage rarely boasted an oven, and the hearth without benefit of chimney, like the Black Houses of the Western Isles of this Century, was the common lot. These were circumstances in which the pot hanging from the swee or bar, and the girdle on the hot embers, reigned supreme, and the culinary results remain part of the continuing tradition to the present day.

The girdle is responsible for much of the rich variety of Tea-breads — the scones and their derivatives which are so characteristic of the Scottish tea-table, and the swee lies behind the strong tradition of one-pot cookery. Its richest legacy is the still-current canon of noble soups which is the chief glory of the Scottish Kitchen, and of the every-day practice of the culinary art in Scottish homes. Less current, but still more than a mere memory, is what may be called one-plate service, in which the plate that has borne its splendid burden of soup receives the meat cooked with the soup. It, like the one-pot cookery, is derived from the swee. Indeed soups like Cullen Skink and Tweed Kettle would elsewhere be recognised as Chowders, and enshrine this ancient Scottish tradition.

The cottage has formed the groundworks of the Scottish Kitchen, but that is not to say the Castle — or the Palace — has made no contribution to the edifice. Their influence lacks the great antiquity of that derived from the pastoral — and bellicose — life of the common people, but is more ancient than is commonly supposed. Dr, Johnson's celebrated account of his Journey to the Western Isles in 1773, often in the context of describing carefully the food he encountered, is at pains to ascribe the "civilising of Scotland" to the then recent English connection. The Grand Cham, though not the last to be so, was mistaken as well as smug.

Scots, at least well know that Mary Queen of Scots and her mother Mary of Guise, brought in their train the French sophistication of the Auld Alliance which remains much in evidence to this day. No doubt it was then that the vocabulary of the Scottish Kitchen became permeated with the French words like *ashet* which are still widely current. And *Soup Lorraine,* and a wealth of exotica among the ingredients of many old recipes, from rice to frangipani, is evidence not only of culinary ambition but of the Continental trade which allowed its realisation. Furthermore, French and Savoyard influence in the Scottish Palace was no new thing in Mary's Sixteenth Century — in the Fifteenth, the Court was already cosmopolitan, reaching a brilliant flowering at the turn of the centuries in the time of James IV. Even then, the Alliance was Auld! Indeed, three centuries earlier, when England suffered Conquest by the Normans, Scotland assimilated a penetration by stealth and dynastic marriage, as recent research suggests, not from Normandy so much as from Flanders and Burgundy, even then more likely to generate sophisticated customs than the cruder freebooters of Normandy.

An historical review such as this would be arid if it did not point at least to the Present, if not the Future. The Present certainly retains ample evidence in the daily practice of Scottish kitchens both public and private, of the influence of the Past. It also has evidence of the continuing openness to cosmopolitan influence, in the ready acceptance of the cuisines from Scotland's latest wave of immigrants, notably Italian, Indian and Chinese. Indeed, discriminating judges have declared Gibson Street in Glasgow to be the Curry House capital of the Western World!

In summary, then the legacy of the Past is a Scots kitchen, which, over and above the special excellence of raw materials created by its Land and the skill of those who work it, is richly endowed with varied traditions expressed in a canon of recipes peculiar to itself. It is also distinguished by practices and skills, still the living birthright, particularly of Scotswomen, which make soup and Tea-bread the chief glories of its practice. And it has raised the High Tea — not itself a peculiarity of Scotland but one shared with many working communities — to the status of a groaning and satisfying Board.

Seeking the characteristically Scottish flavour at that Board, the diner will delight in the *variety* of breads on offer. The morning roll is an especial pleasure in Scotland's towns and cities, often subtly changing in taste and texture as fresh supplies are delivered to shops during the course of the day, until a quite different selection appears in the afternoon. These tea-breads vary not only in taste and texture, but in form as well. At the tea-table there will be pancakes as well as rolls, soda as well as plain scones, plain as well as pan loaves. The fish, especially herring and haddock will rival even the superb beef, and at least in Glasgow, the diner will encounter a near beatification of the plainest of fare, mince, so devoted is the Glaswegian to this dish which is always accceptable. The housewife will have been offered in the shop a range of mince at widely separated prices, the best usually designated "Steak Mince," but as often as not will have selected the meat in the piece and expected to have it minced before her very eyes. Our diner may commonly find it served beneath a poached egg.

He will be unlucky indeed if he does not encounter soup of a most superior kind. Even if it is not one of many soups peculiar to the Scots Kitchen, it will be supplied with vegetables in generous measure and meticulous preparation, and founded on stock which speaks of both tradition and thrift. Bones and poultry carcases are not thrown away in Scotland! And if it is a fish soup, unfamiliar though it may be, he would be foolish to let the opportunity pass.

He will also encounter at many points, the flavour, and above all the texture, of oatmeal. From porridge at breakfast to the oatcakes with cheese at supper, there is scarcely a meal or even a course at which oatmeal does not make its presence felt. Toasted, it adorns and enlivens many a milky sweet, finely or coarsly rolled to taste it far excels breadcrumbs as an adjoint to frying. As well as giving substance to a soup, it will supply the blandest of gruel for the invalid, and equally survival rations for the hardy hill-walker.

Dr. Johnson remarked that wherever a man should have supped, he should arrange to break his fast in Scotland. That traveller would do well to tarry at least until the hour of High Tea!

Burns' Festival — Brown entertains his friend wi' a haggis!

Chapter Four

The Table

*T*he Land provides, the Larder stores, the Kitchen prepares; but it is at the Table that the food is to be enjoyed.

Tables may vary. Some are no more than functional, some decorative; some served and some not; some festive, some plain and everyday. The pleasure the Table offers can be equally as varied — the permutations available from a well-plenished larder are well nigh infinite, the choice made from tham largely a matter of taste. In what has gone before in this survey of what is Scottish about our Scottish Larder and Kitchen, I have been able at least to aspire to an objective presentation of the facts as they appear to my engaged eye. But when the food reaches the Table, personal taste takes over and subjective choice is everything.

What follows, then, is a series of suggestions for bills of fare or menus, it constitutes no Book of the Law demanding slavish observation, but is rather the product of my own taste and feeling for Scottish food.

In the course of my professional life I am often asked to prepare Bills of Fare for particular functions. It is a pleasure to do so, because it means that the company, or at least the organisers of the function, wish to declare their confidence in the Scots Larder, to celebrate it and to enjoy themselves in the process. The first section of this chapter, before a wider selection of suggestions for using Scottish food, contains the Bills of Fare from a few of these functions. In most cases they are accompanied by the brief notes I like to prepare for these occasions in the belief that some indication of the source or origin of the dish to come enhances its enjoyment.

There should be one further word of explanation about two of these Bills of Fare. The first, The Maniory, enshrines in every course an aspect of the Scots Kitchen to which I have already referred, the rich vocabulary of French words which entered Scottish kitchen currency centuries ago and remains in use, some of the words more so than others. The second acknowledges another language, not foreign but more truly native than any other. The Feisd Albannach was prepared for the Gaelic Mod, the great annual festival of the linguistic and musical culture of the Highlands and Islands.

Chapter Five

Some Scottish Recipes

I confess to being somewhat sceptical about recipes. They are, of course, the lodestones to guide the unwary through the reefs and shoals of the perilous seas of cookery, and they do offer at least some assurance against utter disaster. But they provide little certainty of total success and can never be a substitute for the feeling for food and sheer smeddum (*anglice:* gumption) which is the real source of the cook's art, as it is of the pleasures of the diners.

It is in that sense that I offer the following selection. It is certainly not exhaustive, nor is it intended to be authoritative. There is plenty of room for argument about the precise balance of ingredients. How wet is "moist", for instance, as applied to a paste, how brown is "brown" in a sauce? Just a few should, on the other hand, be observed carefully. The prime example is Scotch Broth. If it is not prepared from a mutton stock and if it does not contain barley, and peas, together with a selection of potherbs, though it may be a fine soup, it is not Scotch Broth.

These recipes are based, unless otherwise stated, by kind permission, on the versions given in "British Cookery", published by Croom Helm for the British Farm Produce Council and the British Tourist Authority, following research done for these two bodies at the Scottish Hotel School, University of Strathclyde.

BILLS OF FARE

Lunches

Game Soup

* * * * * * * * * * * * * * * *

Tatties and Herring

* * * * * * * * * * * * * * * *

Whim Wham

* * * * * * * * * * * * * * * *

Tweed Kettle

* * * * * * * * * * * * * * * *

Crowdie & Oatcakes

* * * * * * * * * * * * * * * *

Caledonian Cream

* * * * * * * * * * * * * * * *

Mince & Tatties

* * * * * * * * * * * * * *

Cloutie Dumpling

* * * * * * * * * * * * * *

A Seafood Dinner

Partan Bree

* * * * * * * * * * * * * * *

Queenie Scallops in
a White Wine Sauce

* * * * * * * * * * * * * * *

Baked Halibut

Game Chips   Broccoli

* * * * * * * * * * * * * * * * *

A Lemon Syllabub
With Petticoat Tails

* * * * * * * * * * * * * * *

Finnan Mousse

* * * * * * * * * * * * * * *

Dinners

Loch Fyne Kipper Pate

* * * * * * * * * * * * * * * * *

Scotch Broth

* * * * * * * * * * * * * * * * *

Gigot of Lamb

Clapshot   Braised Leeks

* * * * * * * * * * * * * * * * * * * *

A Fruishie Cream

* * * * * * * * * * * * * * * * * * *

Edinburgh Rock

* * * * * * * * * * * * * * * * * * *

Dinners

Smoked Scotch Salmon

* * * * * * * * * * * * * * * * * *

Old Scots White Soup

* * * * * * * * * * * * * * * * * *

Baron of Beef

* * * * * * * * * * * * * * * * * *

Almond Flory

* * * * * * * * * * * * * * * * * *

Dinners

Cockaleekie

* *

Herring in Oatmeal with
a Mustard Sauce

* * * * * * * * * * * * * * * * * * * *

Roast Rib of Scotch Beef

* * * * * * * * * * * * * * * * * *

Cranachan

* * * * * * * * * * * * * * * * * * *

Haggis   Toasties

* * * * * * * * * * * * * * * * * * *

SECTION 1.   **SOUPS**

Scotch Broth
Hotch Potch
Old Scots White Soup
Cock-a-leekie
Partan Bree
Tweed Kettle
Cullen Cream

SECTION 2.   **FISH**

Loch Fyne Kipper Pate
Tatties & Herrings
Herring in Oatmeal
Haddock with Cheese
Newhaven Cream
Finnan Haddock in Milk

SECTION 3.   **MEAT DISHES**

Boiled Mutton
Mutton Pies (Scotch Pies)
Potted Hough
Aberdeen Sausage
Musselburgh Pie
Venison Collops

SECTION 4.   **VEGETABLE DISHES**

Stovies
Skirlie Tomatoes
Clapshot
Banffshire Potatoes

SOUPS

SCOTCH BROTH

1 lb Neck or Shoulder mutton or lamb
3 oz Pearl barley
Diced Carrots & Turnip)
Diced Onion   )   about 1 lb in total
Sliced leek   )
Dried peas (a small handful)
1 oz fresh chopped parsley
4 pts water
Salt and pepper

Soak peas and barley overnight; strain, bring to boiling point with meat and cold water and simmer for one hour. Skim.

Add diced vegetables and leeks. Season, and cook for a further 2 hours.

Place the parsley in the tureen, and pour on the broth after removing fat.

Fresh veg, such as peas, beans or cauliflower sprigs can be added in season.

SHAKSPEARE A LITTLE ALTERED.

"HE LIVED NOT WISELY, BUT TOO WELL."

HOTCH POTCH *(Serves 6)*

Hotch-Pot is derived from the French term *"hocher"* which means shaking together, plus *"pot"*. Hotch-Potch, hodgepot and hodgepodge are corruptions of the word, indicating a mixture of ingredients.

1 ½ lb neck of lamb or mutton
2½ pints water
Salt and pepper.
3 oz diced turnips
3 oz diced carrots.
3 oz chopped salad onions
2 oz cauliflower
¼ finely chopped lettuce
2 oz green peas
2 oz broad beans
Garnish: chopped parsley

Put the meat in a large pan, add the water and salt and bring to the boil; skim carefully. Add the turnips, carrots and onions, lower the heat and simmer for 2 hours.

Soak the cauliflower and lettuce in cold salted water for 30 minutes; break the cauliflower into sprigs and add with the lettuce to the soup 10 minutes before the end of cooking. Add the peas and beans to the soup for the last 5 minutes.

Lift out the meat, remove skin and bones, dice the meat and return to the soup. Correct seasoning and serve garnished with parsley.

* *

OLD SCOTS WHITE SOUP *(Serves 6-8)*

Dating from the 16th century, this smooth creamy soup is also known as Soup a la Reine. It is traditionally poured over rounds of crusty bread.

1 knuckle of veal.
1 small boiling fowl
2 oz lean bacon
1½ oz chopped carrots
2 oz chopped onions
¼ lb chopped turnips
¼ head chopped celery
1 blade of mace
1 sprig lemon thyme
6 white peppercorns
Salt and pepper
3-4 pt water

Wipe the knuckle of veal with a damp cloth and place in a pan with the fowl and bacon. Add the chopped vegetables, herbs, peppercorns and water; bring to the boil and skim. Season with salt and pepper, then simmer gently for 2 hours, skimming occasionally.

Remove knuckle and chicken. Cut up meat and return to soup. Serve hot over rounds of bread or garnished with vermicelli. Alternatively, leave the soup to cool and set to a jelly. Before reheating, skim off the surface fat and remove any sediments. Reheat and simmer for 30 minutes.

* *

COCK-A-LEEKIE *(Serves 4)*

One of the oldest and best loved dishes of Scotland, cock-a-leekie was traditionally made with an old, tough cock and cooked over a low peat fire overnight for next day's supper.

1 fowl
3 pts beef stock
Faggot of herbs
Salt and pepper
¾-1 lb leeks
6 prunes, soaked overnight

Truss the cock and place in a deep pan with the stock; bring to the boil and skim before adding the herbs, salt and pepper. Prepare the leeks, wash and cut in four lengthways, chop into 1 in. long pieces, keeping the green separate from the white. Add the white of the leeks to the soup and simmer for 2-3 hours.

Add the prunes 30 mins before serving and green of leeks 5 mins before serving. Lift out the cock, remove skin and bones and cut the meat into small pieces; put the meat in a soup tureen, correct seasoning and pour the soup over the meat.

THE POT-HUNTER.

PARTAN BREE *(Serves 4-5)*

"Partan" is the Gaelic word for Crab, and "Bree" is a corruption of "Brigh" meaning broth or juice.

1 large boiled crab
3 oz long grain rice
1 pt milk
1 pt chicken or veal stock
Salt and pepper, anchovy essence
¼ pt double cream

Remove all the meat from the boiled crab, keeping the brown and white meat separate. Cook the rice in the milk mixed with the stock until tender; strain. Sieve or liquidise the rice and brown crab meat.

Reheat the rice and brown crab meat mixture, add the strained milk and stock to the desired consistency, then season with salt, pepper and anchovy essence. Add the chopped white crab meat, stir in the cream and heat the soup through without boiling. Correct seasoning before serving.

* *

TWEED KETTLE *(Serves 3-4)*

A delicious salmon stew, subtly flavoured and easily made from a left-over tail piece of salmon.

1½-2 lb piece of salmon
salt and pepper
ground mace
½ pt fish stock
¼ pt white wine
1½ oz chopped shallots or
      chopped chives to taste
1 oz butter
Garnish: chopped parsley

Simmer the cleaned salmon for 5 minutes in boiling water. Drain and remove skin and bones. Cut the salmon into 2 in. pieces, season with salt, pepper and mace and put in a pan with the fish stock, wine and shallots or chives; simmer for 8 minutes.
Carefully lift out the salmon and place in a serving dish. Reduce the cooking liquid by two thirds; stir in the butter. Pour the sauce over the fish and garnish with parsley.

* *

OUR FRIEND BRIGGS CONTEMPLATES A DAY'S FISHING

CULLEN CREAM *(Serves 4)*

In this version of the traditional Cullen Skink, the soup is thickened by the addition of mashed potatoes and enriched by cream. In the traditional version from Banffshire, the liquor is unthickened and contains substantial pieces of potato and fish.

1 large Finnan haddock
2 oz finely chopped onions
½ pt milk
Salt and pepper
1½-2 oz mashed potatoes
2½ fl oz cream
½ oz butter
Garnish: finely chopped parsley

Skin the haddock and place in a pan with sufficient boiling water to cover. Bring to the boil; add the onion and simmer until the haddock is cooked. Lift out the fish and remove the bones. Return the bones to the stock and simmer for 20 minutes. Flake the fish.

Strain the stock, put in a clean pan and bring to the boil. Boil the milk separately and add to the stock together with the flaked fish. Add salt to taste and simmer for a few minutes. Stir in the potatoes, cream and butter. Correct seasoning. Heat through and serve, garnished with parsley.

* *

FISH

LOCH FYNE KIPPER PATE *(Serves 4)*

The smoked flavour is less pronounced in the kipper than its relation, the bloater, but like the latter it is used in many local variations of fish spreads. The basic flavourings are lemon juice and cayenne, but in one version the usual softened butter is replaced with thick cream and a little olive oil, and in another white wine substitutes lemon juice.

1 Large Loch Fyne Kipper.
5 oz unsalted butter
1 dessertspoon lemon juice
Salt, pepper, cayenne pepper
2 oz clarified butter

Stand the kipper, head down, in a jug of water for 10 minutes. Drain, remove skin and bones. Cut the butter into pieces, set over low heat until half melted, remove from the heat and stir until completely melted. Blend the butter and chopped kipper in a liquidiser to a smooth paste. Season with lemon juice, salt, pepper and cayenne. Pack into small pots and cool; cover with clarified butter.

* *

TATTIES AND HERRINGS (Serves 4)

Reflecting the extreme poverty of former days, this is still a favourite supper dish in Scotland.

4 salt herrings
1½ lb potatoes
Pepper

Put the peeled potatoes in a pan and add water to reach halfway up the potatoes. Wash the herrings and place on top of the potatoes; sprinkle with pepper. Cover the pan with a lid and bring to the boil; simmer gently for about 30 minutes or until the potatoes are cooked.

* *

HERRING WITH OATMEAL (Serves 4)

A favourite way in Scotland of frying herrings and small trout. The cleaned and boned fish may be left whole or cut into fillets. Serve for breakfast, tea or supper, with bannocks and butter, boiled mealy potatoes or oatcakes.

4 · 8 herings
2 oz oatmeal
Salt and pepper
1·2 oz bacon fat.

Allow one or two herrings per portion, depending on size. Season the oatmeal with salt and pepper and coat the herrings. Melt the bacon fat in a frying pan and fry the herrings over gentle heat for 6 minutes on each side. If fillets are used, fry the skin side first.

* *

HADDOCK WITH CHEESE *(Serves 4)*

A substantial lunch or supper dish, ideally accompanied with tiny new potatoes and a cheese sauce.

4 haddock fillets (about 6 oz each)
Lemon juice
Seasoned flour
1 egg
Breadcrumbs
Grated cheese
1½ oz melted butter

Garnish: parsley sprigs, lemon slices

Stuffing: ¼ lb cheese
2 oz fresh white breadcrumbs
1 egg
Salt and pepper

Oven: 350°F; gas mark 4; 20-25 minutes

Wipe the fillets, sprinkle with lemon juice and dust with seasoned flour. For the stuffing mix the grated cheese with the breadcrumbs and parsley; bind with the lightly beaten egg and season with salt and pepper. Divide into four equal portions. Spread the stuffing over the fillets and roll up, securing with wooden cocktail sticks. Brush the rolls with beaten egg and coat with breadcrumbs mixed with grated cheese. Lay the stuffed rolls in a buttered ovenproof dish and pour the melted butter over. Bake in the oven and serve garnished with parsley and lemon.

****

NEWHAVEN CREAM *(Serves 4)*

This is a popular dish in the central lowlands and is usually served hot with parsley, egg or mushroom sauce. In other areas, a similar salmon cream is found. It is made with salmon pounded to a paste, mixed with beaten egg whites and cream, steamed in individual moulds and served with parsley sauce, buttered green peas and toast.

½ lb smoked, cooked and boned haddock
2 oz white breadcrumbs
Salt and pepper
2 oz butter
½ pt milk or single cream
2 eggs

Flake and mash the fish, add breadcrumbs, salt and pepper. Melt the butter in the milk and pour over the mixture; fold in the beaten eggs. Spoon into a well buttered large pudding basin. Cover with foil and steam gently for 1 hour. Remove the foil, turn out the mould and serve.

* *

'This wouldn't be a bad place if the fish would only bite,
and if it wasn't for this confounded wasps' nest.'

FINNAN HADDOCK IN MILK *(Serves 4)*

Finnan haddock takes its name from the little fishing village of Findon in Kincardineshire where the fisherwomen began the now famous cure by hanging salted and dried haddock (known as speldings) in their chimneys to smoke over the peat fires.

1 lb Finnan haddock
½ oz butter
1 teaspoon cornflour
¼ pt milk

Skin the haddock and cut into pieces. Put in a pan with the butter, cover with a lid and steam for 5 minutes. Mix the cornflour with a little milk, stir in the remaining milk. Pour over the fish, bring to the boil and cook for 1 minute until thickened. Lift the fish on to a serving dish, pour over the sauce and serve. A poached egg may be served with each portion.

* *

MEAT

BOILED MUTTON *(Serves 6-8)*

Although mutton is rarely offered for sale now-a-days, this recipe is entirely appropriate to mature hogget, that is to say the previous year's lambs in the early months of the year.

3 lb mutton or hogget
1 faggot of sweet herbs
Salt
½ lb onions, stuck with cloves
4 oz coarse cut carrots
4 oz coarse cut turnips

Wipe the meat and trim off any surplus fat; if necessary tie the meat into shape. Weigh the joint and allow 20-25 minutes per lb plus an extra 20-25 minutes. Put the mutton in a pan, cover with boiling water and add the faggot of herbs; bring to the boil and skim thoroughly. Boil for 5 minutes to harden the outside of the meat; reduce the heat and simmer gently. Season with salt when the mutton is half-cooked.

Thirty minutes before the end of cooking time, add the onions, carrots and turnips. Place the meat on a serving dish surrounded with the vegetables. Use the cooking liquid as the basis for the accompanying sauce, usually caper.

****

MUTTON PIES

1 lb cooked minced mutton
¾ lb hot water crust pastry
½ pt brown sauce
Salt and pepper
Pinch nutmeg
1 egg

Oven: 350°F; gas mark 4; 40 minutes

Mould the warm pie pastry into six individual shapes, about 3½ in. wide and 1½ in. high. Moisten the meat with part of the brown sauce, season with salt, pepper and nutmeg and divide equally between the pie shells.

Cover with pastry lids, make a hole in each and brush with egg. Bake for 40 minutes. Pour warmed brown sauce into the cooked pies before serving them hot.

* *

ALARMING SYMPTOMS AFTER EATING BOILED BEEF
AND GOOSEBERRY PIE.

POTTED HOUGH *(Serves 4)*

Similar to potted head and jellied ox cheek and served in the same manner, with hot toast and a small bowl of fresh lemon juice.

1 lb hough (shin of beef)
1 cow heel or 2 pig trotters
1 oz salt
faggot of herbs
2 whole allspice berries
6 peppercorns
2 cloves
1 blade mace

Cut the hough into small pieces; split the cow heel or trotters down the middle, scald and chop them into pieces. Put the hough and cow heel into a pan with sufficient cold water to cover. Add the salt and herbs and the spices tied in a muslin bag. Bring the water to the boil, cover and simmer gently for 3 hours or until the meat falls off the bones.

Remove the meat and muslin bag, adjust seasoning of the stock and continue to boil until it has reduced and begins to jelly. Chop the meat finely and arrange in a wet mould or basin. Strain the jellied stock over the meat, stirring with a fork to distribute the meat. Leave to set, and turn out before serving.

* *

ABERDEEN SAUSAGE

An economical dish made with uncooked minced beef, shaped into a sausage and boiled. Served cold, cut into slices, with salads or pickles.

1½ lb minced beef
¾ lb fat bacon
6 oz fine oatmeal
½ teaspoon ground mace
½ teaspoon ground nutmeg
Salt and pepper
Brown meat stock

Mince the bacon and mix with oatmeal and beef, season to taste with mace, nutmeg, salt and pepper. Grease a pudding cloth; lay the meat on it shaping it into a sausage about 3 in. by 7 in. Wrap the pudding cloth around it and secure it firmly. Boil the sausage in stock until cooked through, after 2-3 hours. Re-tie the cloth to take up any shrinkage and leave the sausage to cool. Cover the sausage with a meat glaze or browned breadcrumbs. Serve cold.

* *

MUSSELBURGH PIE *(Serves 4)*

¾ lb stewing steak
¼ lb ox or lamb kidney
½ oz seasoned flour
small amount chopped parsley
½ oz dripping
2 oz chopped onions
⅓ pt brown stock
Salt and pepper
6 oz savoury shortcrust, flaky or puff pastry
1 egg
6 chopped oysters
(Also 2 oz sliced mushrooms can be added)

Oven: 400°F; gas mark 6; 1 hour

Cut the steak and kidney into small cubes, dust with seasoned flour and mix with the chopped parsley. Melt the dripping and fry the onions and meat in the fat until light brown. Cover with stock, bring to the boil and simmer gently for 1-1½ hours. Correct seasoning with salt and pepper.

Add the chopped oysters, with their liquid (and mushrooms if desired). Put the meat in a 2 pt pie dish, cover with pastry and brush with beaten egg. Bake in the oven until golden brown.

* *

GLAYVA VENISON CHOPS

Venison Loin Chops
Melted butter

Glayva Parsley Butter:
4 oz butter
1 dessertsp (or to taste) Glayva Liqueur
1 dessertsp blanched, finely chopped parsley
Salt, cayenne and black pepper

Garnish: Watercress

Method:- For the Glayva parsley butter blend the 4 oz butter with liqueur and parsley, season to taste with salt, pepper and cayenne. Shape the butter into a roll, wrap in foil and leave to chill. This quantity will be sufficient for up to 8 chops.

Brush the venison chops on both sides with melted butter. Grill under a moderate heat for 20-25 mins, turning several times and keeping well basted ... season with salt and pepper.

Arrange the chops in a crown on a heated dish and top with pats of Glayva parsley butter. Fill the centre with green peas or fried mushrooms, and garnish with sprigs of watercress.

****

A FRIEND HAS GIVEN MR. BRIGGS A DAY'S SHOOTING.

PHEASANT SHOOTING. A WARM CORNER.

VEGETABLES

STOVIES *(Serves 4)*

1 lb potatoes
½ lb sliced onions
½ oz butter
salt and pepper
¼ pt white stock

Fry the onions lightly in the butter in a pan, add the thickly sliced potatoes, with salt and pepper and stock. Brush the top of the potatoes with butter to prevent them drying out. Bring to the boil, cover and simmer gently for 1 hour.

Small quantities of cooked meat, such as bacon, chicken or mutton, may be added to the pan for the last 15 minutes.

****

SKIRLIE TOMATOES *(Serves 4-5)*

Traditional in Aberdeenshire and Moray, these large tomatoes are stuffed with the oatmeal, onion and suet forcemeat known as Skirlie.

4 large firm tomatoes
Skirlie

Oven: 350°F; gas mark 4; 10-15 minutes

Slice the tops off the washed tomatoes, scoop out the flesh and mix into the prepared skirlie. Drain the tomatoes before stuffing them loosely; replace the tomato lids and bake in the oven for about 15 minutes.

****

CLAPSHOT *(Serves 4)*

½ lb mashed potatoes
½ lb mashed swede turnips
teaspoon chopped chives
1 oz dripping
Salt and pepper

Mix together the hot mashed potatoes and turnips; blend in the chives and dripping. Season to taste with salt and pepper, heat through and serve.

* *

BANFFSHIRE POTATOES *(Serves 4-5)*

4 or 5 jacket baked potatoes
½ oz butter
⅛ teaspoon each, chopped parsley and dried
*   sweet herbs*
Salt and pepper
1½ oz fine white breadcrumbs
¼ beaten egg
2½ fl oz milk

Oven: 425°F; gas mark 7; 20-30 minutes

Slice the top off each potato after baking and scoop out most of the flesh. Mash the potato flesh and mix with butter, parsley and herbs; season to taste with salt and pepper, add the breadcrumbs and egg and blend in the milk.

Return this mixture to the potato skins, replace the lids and re-heat in the oven thoroughly.

* *

SWEETS

BLAIRGOWRIE FOAM *(Serves 4)*

¼ lb sieved raspberry pulp
2 eggs
¼ oz gelatine
Juice of ½ lemon
¼ lb sugar
¼ pt double cream
Toasted nuts, finely chopped

Prepare a souffle dish with a paper collar. Separate the eggs. Dissolve the gelatine in the lemon juice and whisk the egg yolks and sugar to ribbon stage over a pan of warm water. Add the dissolved gelatine and fruit pulp and leave to cool completely.

Whisk the egg whites until stiff and whisk the cream separately. When the gelatine mixture is cold, but before it sets, fold in the whipped cream and the egg whites. Pour the mixture into the souffle dish and leave to set.

Remove the paper collar when the mixture has set and coat the exposed sides with toasted nuts; decorate with whipped cream.

* *

WHIM-WHAM (Serves 4)

¾ pt double cream
2½ fl oz white wine
1½ oz caster sugar
Grated rind of ½ lemon
Sponge fingers
¼ lb red currant jelly
Garnish: crystallised orange or lemon slices

Mix the cream with the wine, sugar and lemon rind and beat until frothy. Spoon one third of this mixture into individual serving dishes, put a few sponge fingers over the cream and cover with a layer of jelly.

Arrange another layer of cream, sponge and jelly and finish with the remaining cream. Decorate with orange or lemon slices and chill.

* *

CRANACHAN (Serves 4)

This dish used to be traditional at Hallowe'en, and charms would be folded into the cream mixture; each charm had a particular significance; a ring indicated marriage, a button bachelorhood, a thimble spinsterhood, a coin wealth and a horse shoe good luck.

3-4 oz oatmeal
½ pt double cream
2 oz caster sugar
1¼ fl oz rum or a few drops vanilla essence
Garnish: ripe, soft berries

Toast the oatmeal lightly under the grill or in a thick frying pan and leave to cool completely. Whip the cream until stiff, sweeten to taste with sugar and add the rum or vanilla essence.

Stir in the oatmeal and spoon the cream into serving dishes. Decorate with fresh berries. Chill and serve.

* *

EDINBURGH FOG *(Serves 4)*

½ pt double cream
½ tablespoon caster sugar
Vanilla essence
2 oz ratafia biscuits
1 oz chopped almonds

Sweeten the cream with sugar and vanilla essence to taste. Beat until stiff and fold in the biscuits and almonds. Spoon into glasses and serve chilled.

* *

SCOTS FLUMMERY *(Serves 4-5)*

1 oz currants
2½ fl oz dry sherry or white wine
½ pt milk
2½ fl oz double cream
4 egg yolks
1½ oz sugar
½ dessertspoon rose water
Pinch grated nutmeg

Soak the currants in the sherry for at least 1 hour. Heat the milk and cream; pour this over the beaten eggs and sugar; mix and strain. Add the rose water and nutmeg and cook in a double saucepan until thickened.

Stir in the soaked currants and sherry and spoon the custard into small dishes to set.

* *

PUDDINGS & TARTS

ALMOND FLORY (FLORENTINE TART)

A fashionable tart in Edinburgh's Golden Age.

Grind finely together:-

1 lb blanched almonds
8 egg yolks
4 egg whites
½ lb clarified butter
1 lb of currants

Season with sugar, cinnamon and nutmeg to taste and add ½ pt cream and some whisky or brandy to taste and candied peel if desired.

Mix thoroughly and bake lightly in a puff pastry double tart.

* *

EDINBURGH TART *(Serves 4)*

¼ lb sweet or rich shortcrust pastry
1 oz butter
1 oz caster sugar
1 oz chopped candied peel
¼ oz sultanas
1 oz flour
1 egg

Oven: 375°F; gas mark 5; 30-40 minutes

Line an 8 in. flan ring, set on a baking sheet, with the pastry.

Melt the butter and add the sugar, peel, sultanas and flour; remove from the heat and stir in the beaten egg. Pour the mixture into the pastry case and bake for about 40 minutes.

CLOUTIE DUMPLING

"Clout" (pronounced "Cloot") is the Scottish term for a cloth.

1 lb flour
4-6 oz breadcrumbs
½ lb sugar
½ lb finely chopped suet
½ lb sultanas
½ lb currants
4 oz muscatel raisins
4 oz chopped peel
2 grated apples or carrots
1 teaspoon baking powder
½ teaspoon salt
2 teaspoons each, cinnamon, spice and ginger
2 eggs
½ lb black treacle
Milk

Mix together the flour, breadcrumbs, sugar, suet, dried fruits, apples, baking powder, salt and spices. Blend the beaten eggs with the treacle and stir into the dry mixture, with enough milk to give a soft dough.

Put the mixture in a floured pudding cloth and tie the ends; alternatively, spoon into a 3 pt greased pudding basin and tie down with buttered greaseproof paper and foil or cloth. Steam for 3-4 hours.

* *

URNEY PUDDING *(Serves 4)*

2 oz sugar
2 oz butter
1 beaten egg
2 oz plain flour
Pinch salt
3 oz red jam

Beat the sugar and butter until light and creamy, beat in the eggs and fold in the sifted flour and salt. Mix the jam lightly into this mixture to give a marbled effect.

Grease a 2 pt pudding basin and pour in the mixture; cover with greaseproof paper and steam for 1½-2 hours. Turn out and serve with jam sauce.

* *

GROSET FRUSHIE

A frushie is described by Marion McNeill as being long popular in the West of Scotland. It is a fruit tart in which the pastry-top is formed into a lattice of half inch strips. Half the strips are laid at intervals across the filled tart, the other half across them, interwoven. The interweaving can best be done on waxed paper, the whole then turned over onto the tart, and brushed with a sugar-and-water glaze before bakiing.

Any fruit may be used, apple, groset (gooseberry) and black or red currants being particularly favoured.

Serve with cream.

* *

TEA BREADS & CAKE

SCOTS PANCAKES

¾ pt milk
2 eggs
5 oz sugar or 2 tbs Golden Syrup
2 oz oil or melted butter
1 lb plain flour
1 oz baking powder
Pinch salt

Beat together the milk, eggs, sugar, oil or melted butter; fold in the flour, sifted with baking powder and salt. Mix to a soft dropping consistency.

Drop the batter in spoonfuls on to a heated griddle and cook until bubbles appear on top, then turn and cook on the other side. Serve hot or cold, with butter and jam.

(Traditionally made with soured or butter-milk, baking soda and cream of tartar.)

* *

HIGHLAND SLIM CAKES

1 lb plain flour
4 oz butter
2 eggs
Hot milk

Sift the flour, rub in the butter and add the beaten eggs. Mix with milk to give an elastic dough. Roll out, ½ in. thick, and cut into rounds; bake on a hot griddle, cooking each side for 4-5 minutes.

****

SELKIRK BANNOCKS

3 lb plain flour
1 tablespoon salt
1 oz fresh yeast
¾ lb sugar
1½ pt water
¾ lb melted butter and lard
1¼ lb sultanas or
1 lb sultanas and 4 oz currants
6 oz finely chopped orange peel

Oven: 425°F; gas mark 7; 1½ hours

Sift the flour and salt and add the yeast, creamed with a little sugar and a little of the warm water; mix to a dough with the remaining water. Knead thoroughly and set to rise and double.

Knock the dough back, knead and work in the butter and lard, sugar, dried fruit and peel. Shape, put into large round greased tins and set to prove. Bake for about 1½ hours.

****

DUNDEE CAKE

1 lb butter
1 lb caster sugar
9 eggs
1 lb plain flour
6 oz currants
6 oz raisins
6 oz sultanas
4 oz chopped mixed peel
Grated rind of 1 orange
2 oz blanched, split almonds

Oven: 350°F; gas mark 4; 2 hours

Cut the butter into small pieces and cream with the sugar until light and fluffy; beat the eggs in a bowl set over a pan of hot water and whisk into the creamed mixture. Fold in the sifted flour, alternately with the currants, raisins, sultanas, mixed peel and orange rind.

Turn into a double-lined, greased 9-10 in. cake tin and arrange the almonds over the top in circular patterns. Bake in the oven for 2 hours.

* *

FOCHABERS GINGERBREAD

½ lb butter
4 oz caster sugar
½ lb black treacle
1 pt beer
1 lb plain flour
½ teaspoon bicarbonate of soda
2 teaspoons each, ground ginger and mixed spice
1 teaspoon each, ground cinnamon and cloves
4 oz sultanas
4 oz currants
3 oz finely chopped candied peel
3 oz ground almonds

Oven: 350°F; gas mark 3; 3 hours

Line and grease a round, 10 in. wide, shallow cake tin; sprinkle lightly with flour.

Cream the butter and sugar until light and fluffy; dissolve the treacle in the beer and sift the flour, bicarbonate of soda and the spices. Fold the flour into the creamed mixture, alternately with the treacle and beer; add the sultanas, currants, candied peel and ground almonds.

Pour into the prepared tin and bake for about 3 hours.

* *

PLAIN COOKIES

1 lb plain flour
2 teaspoons salt
½ oz fresh yeast
3 oz sugar
4 oz butter
2½ fl oz milk
3 eggs
1 beaten egg

Oven: 425°F; gas mark 7; 10 minutes

Sift the flour and salt, add the yeast creamed with the sugar, and the butter melted in the warm milk; blend in the three beaten eggs and mix to a soft dough. Knead on a floured surface and set aside to rise and double in size.

Knock the dough back and divide it into 2 oz pieces shaping them into rounds. Set on a greased baking tray and prove. Brush with egg and bake.

* *

BISCUITS Etc.

SHORTBREAD

14 oz plain flour
2 oz rice flour
½ lb butter
¼ lb caster sugar
Pinch of salt

Oven: 425°F; gas mark 7; 5 minutes
325°F; gas mark 3; 30-40 minutes

Place the butter and sugar on a board and knead until thoroughly blended. Sift the flour and rice flour with a pinch of salt over the board and gradually work these into the butter and sugar. Keep the butter cool by ideally working the mixture on a marble slab.

When all the flour is incorporated, shape the dough into ½ in. thick and 8 in. wide rounds with the hand or a shortbread mould. Pinch the edges neatly all round with the finger and thumb; set on greased baking trays and prick closely with a fork. The mixture may also be shaped into strips and cut into fingers.

Bake in a hot oven, reducing the temperature after 5 minutes. Leave to cool before removing from the trays or tins, sprinkle with sugar.

* *

AYRSHIRE SHORTBREAD

4 oz butter
4 oz plain flour
4 oz rice flour
2 oz caster sugar
1 egg
1 tablespoon cream

Oven: 350°F; gas mark 4; 30 minutes

Rub the butter into the sifted flour; add the rice flour and mix to a stiff dough with the egg and cream. Knead well and turn out on a floured board; roll out, ¾ in. thick, and cut into rounds with a 2½ in. cutter.

Set on greased baking trays, prick with a fork and bake. Sprinkle with sugar while still hot.

* *

PETTICOAT TAILS

These little biscuits are cut like a full, hooped petticoat, the centre of the dough being cut out to avoid points on the brittle biscuits.

½ lb butter
6 oz icing sugar
¾ lb plain flour
Water
Caster sugar

Oven: 325°F; gas mark 3; 30-40 minutes

Cream the butter and sifted icing sugar, fold in the flour and mix to a stiff dough with water. Roll out to a round, ¼ in. thick. Cut out a small circle from the centre with a tumbler and remove; cut the outer circle into eight wedges, bake for 30-40 minutes and dust with caster sugar.

* *

CRULLA

2 oz butter
2 oz caster sugar
2 eggs
¾ lb self raising flour

Cream the butter and sugar together until light and fluffy. Beat the eggs and whisk into the creamed mixture; add the sifted flour and mix to a soft dough.

Roll the mixture out, ¼ in. thick, and cut into lengths, 5 in. long and ½ in. wide; cut each piece into three strips; plait together and deep-fry in hot fat at 325°F until light brown, turning once. Drain on absorbent paper and dredge with sugar.

* *

OATCAKES

½ tablespoon melted fat
¼ teaspoon salt
½ teaspoon bicarbonate of soda
½ lb fine oatmeal
Lukewarm water

(Reduce the quantities according to the size of the griddle)

Add the fat, salt and bicarbonate of soda to the oatmeal, mix with enough lukewarm water to make a stiff but pliable dough. Roll out in oatmeal, ⅛ in. thick.

Cut the dough round a dinner plate to make one large round and cut this into quarters; alternatively, cut the rolled-out mixture into small rounds or triangles.

Bake on a fairly hot griddle, for 5 minutes, turning once; finish off in a hot oven for a few minutes.

* *

PARLIES
(SCOTTISH PARLIAMENT CAKES)

4 oz black treacle
4 oz butter
½ lb plain flour
2 teaspoons ground ginger
4 oz soft brown sugar

Oven: 325°F; gas mark 3; 30-40 minutes

Melt the treacle and butter over gentle heat, fold in the sifted flour and ginger and add the sugar.

Mix to a stiff dough and roll out very thinly. Set on greased baking trays, mark in squares and bake. Separate the squares while still warm.

* *

Resting on the road to the harvest

The Fare

by
John Leese

Since it was first conceived in 1981, our Bill of Fare has undergone many revisions. Battered by vile weather, constrained by the busy schedules of our guests, fortified by the generosity stimulated by our twin purposes, it is set before you with a suitable combination of pride in this Scottish product which animates each course, and the humble faith that your palates will be massaged as your pockets are charitably lightened.

'Overture and Beginners' expresses some of the constraints and the generosity. Cold consommé speaks of hope of warmer weather but also of the rich resources of game which still stock the Scottish larder.

The trout is at once a commemoration and an aspiration. The Howietoun Trout Farm was established a century ago by the remarkable Scotsman, Sir John Maitland. Today it carries the hope, based on his foundation, of the reinstatement of the stock of the superlative Loch Leven brown trout by Stirling University Institute of Aquaculture. It is the foundation stock of their programme which we hope you will enjoy today.

Aberdeen-Angus beef has been carried by the skill of Scottish stocksmanship to the four corners of the earth. Today's barons of beef, presented in the interests of simplicity in the abbreviated form of this great cut — the Double Sirloin — have their origin in the heartland of the great beef breed of Scotland in Aberdeenshire. The Madeira in the sauce recalls a long-standing affection for the fruits of warmer southern climes in our Scottish culinary tradition.

The Scottish kitchen is no narrow parochial thing, nor yet the Scottish larder. Our tartlet celebrates the oldest of our international connections by combining Scottish raspberries and French Cognac, each the *sans pareil* of its kind.

Our cheese board expresses the widening variety of texture and flavours which are increasingly becoming available from Scotland.

The final delicacy is a personal self-indulgence, now shared, sweetmeats long enjoyed in the bosom of my family in a remote Argyllshire clachan.

TASTE OF SCOTLAND

MENU

Kipper Mousse with whisky
served with hot oatcakes

* * *

Hairst Bree

* * *

Sirloin of Beef Cooked on the Bone
with Horseradish Sauce

Selection of Fresh Vegetables
New Potatoes

* * *

Raspberry Burnt Cream

* * *

Scottish Cheeses
served with the four malts of Scotland

Oatcakes and French Bread

* * *

Coffee

WINES

Pouilly Blanc Fume 1982
Chateau Malartic la Graviere 1970

KIPPERS, smoked, split herring, have been made in Scotland for at least two centuries and are particularly featured on many Scottish breakfast tables.

HAIRST, OR HARVEST BREE or soup is a traditional Scottish soup utilising any and all of the wide range of vegetables available at harvest time.

The Roast Beef of Old England is traditionally Scottish! Since the end of the Eighteenth Cedntury the most highly prized beef In the English markets was brought on foot or by sea from Aberdeen and it was there that the highly refined beef breed, the Aberdeen Angus was developed.

RASPBERRIES are the Scottish fruit par excellence. Centred on the area north of the River Tay, the Scottish raspberry industry represents two-thirds of the E.E.C. crop.

SCOTTISH CHEESES have taken many forms through the centuries. The soft cream and skimmed milk cheeses had their origin in the cottage, and the hard pressed cheeses have developed from the Dunlop type first recorded in the Seventeenth Century in the south-west of Scotland.

OATCAKES are a much-loved item on every Scottish table, with an almost talismanic significance.

International PEN Conference Edinburgh 1970

Gammon and Crowdie Rolls

Cullen Skink

Haggis

Roast Rib of Aberdeen Angus Beef
Baked Potatoes Yorkshire Pudding
Brussels Sprouts

Blairgowrie Flam

Scapa Queens

Helensburgh Toffee Edinburgh Rock

Cheese Board

Coffee

*Niersteiner Gutes Domthal Gustav Adolf Schmitt 1968/69 /
Beaune Geisweiler & Fils 1966 / Drambuie / Courvoisier VSOP*

As a starter, served cold, rolls of thinly sliced gammon filled with Crowdie, the traditional Highland cottage cheese.

Cullen Skink, a regional soup from the shores of the Moray Firth, deserves a place with the great dishes of the world. The stock is made by simmering Finnan-Haddie (smoked haddock) with chopped onions. Milk is added and the fish is flaked back into the stock. The soup is then thickened and finally blended with butter.

There's not enough space to tell you all about Haggis. Just enjoy it, served here in the popular way with mashed potato and turnip.

Aberden Angus beef needs no advertisement. Here is a thick slice cut from the roasted rib, with a potato baked in foil, split and filled with sour cream and chives. We could have insisted on accuracy and called the extras Batter Pudding and Musselburgh Sprouts but we deferred to the International character of the occasion.

Flam, an egg custard, is one of the many reminders in the Scots kitchen of our Auld Alliance with France. Tonight's version celebrates the area north of the Tay where three-quarters of Britain's raspberries are grown.

These queen scallops are harvested from Scapa Flow. Served in their shells as a savoury, the scallops have been gently poached and are dressed with a white wine sauce.

A Scottish cheese board can nowadays encompass a range of flavours and textures to rival any. It is there on your table throughout the evening so that you can select a taste for each mood of the meal.

Helesburgh Toffee is really Tablet. And Tablet is a much-loved Scots sweetmeat made from sugar, condensed milk, butter and flavourings.

Edinburgh Rock is exported round the world. It is not hard and brittle as the name might suggest but dissolves to instant sweetness in the mouth.

Our climate has made us tasters of wine rather than producers. So the wines come from Germany and France. But the Drambuie is all Scottish.

SCOTTISH
BUSINESS ACHIEVEMENT
AWARD 1982

Wines

The Bill of Fare

Pheasant and Cucumber Jelly

Nederburg Fonternel, 1980

* * *

Howietoun Brown Trout

* * *

Baron of Aberdeen-Angus Beef
in Madeira Sauce

Mildara Cabernet Sauvignon,
Coonawarra, Estate Bottled,
1976

Clyde Valley Salad

Nettle and Turnip Purée

Château Fourcasa Hosten,
C. B. Listrac, 1976

Scottish Potatoes

* * *

Auld Alliance Tartlet

* * *

A Scottish Cheese Board
with

Scotch Whisky

Oatmeal Bannocks

* * *

Coffee

The Scottish Woollen Industry and The Fabrex Exhibition

THE ANNUAL TEXTILE DINNER

8th October 1985

MENU

Flambeau d'Alsace 1983	**CULLEN CREAM** *A creamed fish soup of Finnan Haddie*
	* * *
	APPLE SORBET *A light, toothful intermission.*
	* * *
Chateau Plaisance 1982	**LOIN OF SCOTCH LAMB** *Loin of Lamb with an oatmeal stuffing, served with a whisky-enriched gravy.*
	* * *
	CREAM OF THE CARSE AND CLARET *Stiffly whipped Cream Nests filled with Raspberries marinated in Claret.*
	* * *
Taylors late-bottled vintage reserve Port	**A SCOTTISH CHEESEBOARD** *A selection of Scottish Cheeses with traditional Highland Oatcakes.*
	* * *
Tamnavoulin 10 year old unblended Glenlivet Malt Whisky or Glayva Liqueur	**COFFEE AND A DRAM**

The Loyal Toast will be proposed by Mr George Kynoch, Chairman of the Scottish Woollen Publicity Council.

Feisd Albannach

Fàilte is Furan

        Crowdie Dip

★

Buntàta is Adag phronn

        Finnan & Tatties

★

Asna Uain le Osan

        Lamb Cutlets

★

Measan is Cé Reòta

        Grampian Snow

★

Caise
Cofaidh agus Drama

★

Brot

The assistance of W. A. Baxter & Sons, Brechin Bros. and
Tomatin Distillery is gratefully acknowledged

An Comunn Gaidhealach

Rogha Ciuil — Rogha Bidhe
Da thiodhlac anns a bheil Alba
beairteach.

Tha An Comunn Gaidhealach is
Comhairle Toraidh nan Tuathanach
am Breatann toilichte a bhith
a' co-oibreachadh ann a bhith
a' cumail na Feisd so aig
Fosgladh a' Mhoid an 1969.

Good Music — Good Food.
Two gifts with which Scotland is
generously endowed.

An Comunn Gaidhealach and
the British Farm Produce Council
are happy to combine in celebrating
them in this Feast to mark the
opening of the National Mod, 1969.

BRITISH FARM PRODUCE COUNCIL
and
NORTH OF SCOTLAND MILK MARKETING BOARD

MANIAIRIA   A MANIORY

Original French

Doublier

THE DUBLAR

———

Hochepot

HOTCH POTCH

———

Broche: gigot

BROTCHED GIGOT OF LAMB

Assiette

AN ASHET OF VEGETABLES

Tarte-en-puree

TARTAN PURRY

Groseille

GROSSET SAUCE

———

Ananas: flan

ANANAS FLAM

with

Petite gatelles

PETTICOAT TAILS

——— ———

Quelque choses

KICKSHAWS

———

Bon aller

A BONALLY

———